The Ultimate Beginner's Guide to Making Money with Domain Flipping

A Simple, Practical, and Risk-Free System for Buying and Selling Domain Names Online

By
Howard Cayce

Table Of Contents

INTRODUCTION TO DOMAIN FLIPPING............9

DOMAIN SELECTION 101.................................15

THE TRUTH ABOUT AGED DOMAINS.............27

PROFITABLE DOMAIN PARKING.....................35

THE VALUE IN DROPPED DOMAINS...............41

BACKORDERING DOMAIN NAMES.................45

DOMAIN FLIPPING SYSTEM............................49

DOMAIN TASTING 59

CONCLUSION: FINAL TIPS AND ADVICE.......63

TOOLS & RESOURCES.................................... 67

LEGAL NOTICE

The Publisher has strived to be as accurate and complete as possible in the creation of this report, notwithstanding the fact that he does not warrant or represent at any time that the contents within are accurate due to the rapidly changing nature of the Internet.

While all attempts have been made to verify information provided in this publication, the Publisher assumes no responsibility for errors, omissions, or contrary interpretation of the subject matter herein. Any perceived slights of specific persons, peoples, or organizations are unintentional.

In practical advice books, like anything else in life, there are no guarantees of income made. Readers are cautioned to reply on their own judgment about their individual circumstances to act accordingly.

This book is not intended for use as a source of legal, business, accounting or financial advice. All readers are advised to seek services of competent professionals in legal, business, accounting, and finance field.

Introduction To
Domain Flipping

Do you have $10.00 to spare? If you do, you can jump into the world of domain (DN) flipping and start generating a profit on Day One. It's a no brainer technique that is being used by hundreds of domain flippers around the world who are pulling in tons of quick cash from simple domain flips.

And don't worry about finding brandable, in demand domain names. While we certainly will never likely find a one word domain name available anywhere online (for less than a coupe of hundred thousand dollars), we can still make a decent, and steady income flipping average domain names found on expired lists, or available for immediate registration with your regular domain service provider!

The potential for ongoing profit is truly unlimited, and you can average anywhere from $50.00 in profit, to $200.00 or more. Best of all, there are ways to safeguard your domain investments so that you NEVER lose money on a domain sale or auction.

The very worst-case scenario? *You break even.*

Buying and selling domain names can be an exceptionally lucrative venture to get into, however if you are starting off with very little cash flow, it's always best to purchase lower cost domains and generate small profits as you work your way up to larger flips.

I have sold hundreds of domain names that I secured from marketplaces like Ebay and resold on marketplaces like NamePros.com, Flippa.com or DNForum.com.

While the marketplaces where domain sales are most lucrative are different from that of website flipping, the flip process remains the same with your focus being on locating and purchasing low cost domains and selling them for a higher price.

One of the great aspects of domain flipping is that the work required is minimal. Unlike website flipping, you aren't forced into updating websites, tweak or split test sales copy or outsource tasks to freelancers. You can start, run and manage your domain flipping business entirely on your own with minimal start up costs involved.

To get started in the domain selling arena, all you need to do is find memorable, appealing domain names in niche markets and sell them to buyers, eager to create their own website because they see value in the domains you are selling.

And don't be mistaken. Even standard, $10 domain registrations can be sold for up to 10x the initial cost if you are able to present the domain name to potential buyers in such a way that you give them ideas as to how to develop the domain and emphasize branding opportunities.

In fact, I've seen "aged' domains that were registered for $9 that had absolutely no revenue or traffic sell for up to $2000 simply because the buyer had a great idea for the domain name and felt it would fit in with their existing brand.

Furthermore, the risks are quite low as are the investment costs, and once you have set up your system so that you are generating daily profits, it will require no more than one hour a day to keep the cash flow going.

Many of my partners, students and friends are earning $500 - $2,500 per week from flipping low cost domain names, while others have gone to secure high value domain names that are generating them revenue even before they are resold.

It's not a difficult business to get into, if you follow my simple guide to buying and selling domain names.

To start, you will want to create accounts at the following domain 'hot spot', where you can both buy and sell domain names:

www.Flippa.com
http://forums.digitalpoint.com
http://www.eBay.com
http://www.DNForum.com
http://www.NamePros.com

Domain Selection 101

When it comes to finding the best domain names, the easiest route to take is in exploring the expired domain listings that consist of domains that were previously registered but were not renewed.

These kinds of domains are far more appealing to buyers due to the fact that they are considered 'aged', despite the fact that they have expired and are no longer active. In most cases, if you register the domain shortly after it expires, you'll be able to maintain any existing traffic or page rank that the domain already has, and when it comes to domains, age, backlinks, traffic and page rank add incredible value to what the domain is worth within the marketplaces.

I use a few different resources when locating expired domain names including: www.WSMDomains.com and http://www.RedHotDomainNames.com

With either of these resources, you are able to access and download complete listings of both expired domain names as well as domains that are about to expire so that you can receive an alert when the domain is dropped into the market and grab it before someone else does!

When it comes to securing aged domains from drop lists, you'll want to actively download lists of expired domain names every single day, and run them through a filtering script, such as the one available at:

www.alouwebdesign.ca

Another filtering tool is available at: www.DomainPunch.com/products/domainfilter and it's entirely free.

What this script will do is enable you to sort through the listings of domains by extension, as well as weed through domains that have numbers or hyphens. And since you'll be sifting through thousands of domain names, using a software utility that will sort the names for you, will save a lot of time.

These services are quite flexible in how you can set it up to filter through these lists for you, choosing between extensions, hypenated domains or even domains with specific keywords.

They can also handle very large text based lists so even if you are interested in sorting through thousands of potential domains, the software can handle it!

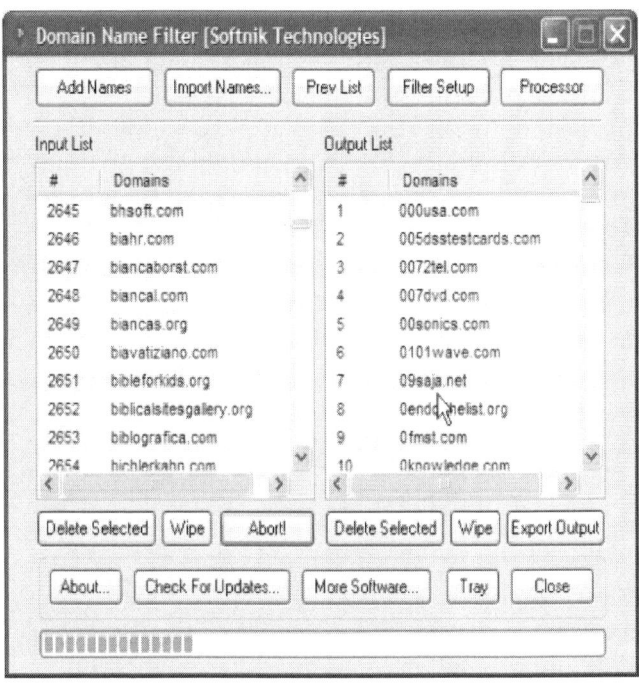

Download and install the software and check it out so you're familiar with how it works and what features are available. You will find it will save you an incredible amount of time and make the job easier and more enjoyable, plus by using an automated system to browse domains, you'll give yourself an edge over the competition, as you'll be able to find quality domains faster and easier – and with less work involved.

When it comes to purchasing domain names for resale, you want to stick with the top level extension, the dot com, and avoid any domains with numbers, or other characters. While other domains with alternative extensions can be valuable, you'll minimize your risks of a domain not selling if you stick to the top level extension when just starting out. Once you've gained experience in the domain flipping arena, you can consider buying and selling other domain types.

You will also want to focus on searching for expired domain names that are as short as possible, and with utilities such as the one available at alouwebdesign.ca, you are able to search through your lists by setting a maximum and minimum length, meaning that you can sort through the domains so that only ones that are shorter will appear.

Personally, I set the maximum length to 20 characters and of course, the minimum to zero, so that it includes the shortest domain names on my expired lists.

You will also need to enter in specific keywords, these are words that when contained within any of the expired domains, will be included in the results page after you have entered in your list and filtered through the results.

Creating a keyword swipe file is an ongoing job, and one that you should concentrate a lot of effort on, as the more prime keywords you enter into the software, the better your chances of finding true gems.

This comes down to the niche markets you cater to, and you should take a bit of time to start creating a list of keywords in a text file that you can copy and paste into the software.

Apart from targeted keywords, you should also consider thinking outside the box a bit, by drumming up a list of memorable keywords that when added to a domain can be used for branding purposes.

I've sold countless domain names contrived of two keywords that really made no sense together but because of the sound, the appeal and the brandability factor, they were gobbled up quickly.

Think about some of the Internet's most popular websites like Twitter.com, Facebook.com or FeedBurner.com whose domains are off the beaten path but definitely memorable, which is one of the best important elements of a domain names profitability.

Take some time to get familiar with both the expired domain websites as well as the software available to help you manage the lists and weed through potential gems.

Once you have sorted through your lists, it's time to run the remaining domains through a bulk domain registration tool, to determine what domains are still available, as others downloading these lists may have scooped up a few already.

One great resource for checking large domain lists for availability is available at www.Moniker.com where you can enter in hundreds of domain names and allow the software to validate whether the domains are available or have been registered.

With Moniker, you can check up to 500 domains at once, which will free up a lot of your time so you can continue searching for solid and available domain names.

You can visit Monikers bulk domain registration page at:

http://www.Moniker.com/domains/batch_reg.jsp

On this page you will see the following form:

Step 1: Enter domains	Register Multiple Domains (500 Domains Max)
To start bulk domain registration, enter or cut and paste the domain names you wish to check, one domain name per line.	
An example of bulk domain registration:	
Domain1.com Domain2.net Domain3.info	
You can also enter the domains without an extension and pick them in step two.	☑ **Automatically renew the registration of these domain.(Highly Recommended)**
You can select from existing categories or enter a NEW Category for all domains registered.	**Registration Years:** 1 ▼
	Category: DEFAULT » Select Existing Categories

Once you have a solid listing of available domain names, it's time to follow the advice of many who have garnered wealth in the domain industry for many years through proper and careful selection.

Copy and paste a portion of your domains from your list into the text box. Remember, it can only check 500 at a time.

Once you have entered them in, click the Search tab to send your query off. Wait a few minutes for the results. (This can sometimes take a few minutes, so be patient).

When checking for domain names you can choose to have Moniker search for only dot com extensions which is what you should focus on primarily, when you are new to domain names.

Dot com (.com) is the most popular extension and are often easier to flip.

For other extensions, you will be required to do more in depth keyword and traffic research so let's stick to .com's for now.

Once Moniker is done searching for the domain names you have entered in, you will see a results window where you can choose to register them with Moniker.

Note that you are not required to register them there, you can use whatever domain registration provider you wish, we are simply using Monikers bulk domain checker to sort through our lengthy list to determine availability of each domain name.

For me, I typically register a handful of domain names a day; I never go overboard unless I happen to stumble upon a great list or a good deal.

When you are first starting out, you should set aside $50.00 and try to register 5 domain names to start.

Once you have begun to generate a profit and have a feel for how domain flipping works, you can begin to take a portion of your profits and invest it back into registering domain names.

It will not take long before you have the business paying for itself entirely, including higher priced domain names that you will eventually register and flip.

You can also find tons of expired domain lists on domain forums and blogs. I have included quite a few within the Resources section at the end of this guide, so be sure to check those out.

Whenever you download an expired list of domains, you should begin to weed through it taking notes of the ones that appeal to you either because they are short, memorable or based on keywords that you have found to be in demand.

The only problem with expired domain listings are

that if you don't move quickly, a lot of the better domain names will be snatched up as these lists tend to get distributed all over the Internet rather quickly.

Another obstacle when browsing through expired domain lists is the fact that often times domain registrars such as GoDaddy.com, will snag any domains that have existing traffic.

This means that some of the domain names on the lists will not become available after they have expired, but instead, held by the domain registrars for a period of 5-7 days before potentially being dropped and made available again.

The best way to address this is to go over each lists (and as many different lists as you can), taking notes of any domain names that are appealing.

Write them down in a text file and every day, take a few minutes to check whether the domains have become available to the public.

Before you do this however, you should know that there are many domain registrars online that will literally steal your domain research.

What this means is that when you type the domain name into your browser to see if it's available, or if you visit a domain registrar's website and enter in a domain to see its status, these companies analyze this data and may snap up a domain you are considering.

This has been happening for many years and has recently caused quite a stir amongst the domain community when some well-known registrars were caught doing this.

To avoid domain snatching, I recommend using a trusted provider, such as www.DomainTools.com managed by Jay Westerdal.

Jay has a strict policy against domain research stealing, so you can rest assured that if you use his service to check for domains, you will not be exposing your considerations to someone waiting to snatch it up.

www.Verisign.com is also another trusted provider, and despite allegations regarding NameCheap from time to time, I have used them for many years without any problems in having my potential domains gobbled up or squatted on by their team.

They are also my chosen registrar due to their lower prices and included WHO privacy protection guard that comes free with every domain registratration.

The Truth About Aged Domains

Domains that have been registered and never dropped are called "Aged Domains".

These domains typically sell for more than a new one does because it has been around for awhile, it's usually out of the Google Sandbox and for those who are looking for aged domains, it can help them develop an existence online, a history, or credibility in their niche markets simply because if the domain has been around for years, it appears that they have as well.

Aged domains can also be found on forums like DNForum.com and simply by typing in the keywords "Aged Domains" into the search bar you can easily locate domain auctions that include these older domain names.

I have purchased dozens of domain names for $40 or less that were anywhere from 5 – 10 years old. Just based on the age alone I was able to flip these domain names for over 5x what I paid.

For instance, one domain name I purchased was never used, meaning it had never featured a website on it, it just sat parked in the users account for over six years.

I purchased the domain for only $30.00 and because of its age, I was able to flip it for $379.00.

That's quite a boost in profit from a domain I paid so little for.

While there is no exact science as to what type of domain names will ultimately be worth the most, apart from the obvious short and memorable domain names, there are a few things to keep in mind:

1) Development Potential

When you analyze the available domains in your list, consider what each domain name could represent and be used for when creating a website presence.

An example of which is whether the domain name is one that could represent a product title, or better served as a personal portfolio, a social community, a directory or perhaps a forum.

While the purpose of the domain name will unlikely match your ideas when it is sold, by thinking of a clear purpose for each domain name will not only help you make sound choices during the selection process, but can also be included in the domain auction, as a way of passing on the ideas to prospective buyers who are considering purchase.

2) Length

It can not be said enough, that the length of a domain name, apart from the odd occurrence where you locate a lengthy domain name that still carries with it, a memorable element, most of the domain names you purchase should be relatively short, basically consisting of two words.

3) Trademark Issues

Avoid registering any domain names that could infringe upon the trademark of existing companies, whether or not you believe that the company will take action or not should not be considered.

The last thing you want is to purchase a domain name that is unable to be sold due to buyers being cautious or concerned of building a website on a domain that ends up being seized by a company wishing to protect their identity.

4) Relevant / Popular Keywords

Does the domain name contain popular keywords that are used by those seeking out more information in search engines? If so, your domain name just increased its value instantly.

One of the easiest ways to determine whether a

keyword is a common one is by using the free service available at www.SEOBook.com or www.Overture.com

5) Existing Traffic

If you are purchasing aged or recently expired domains, you will want to determine whether there is existing traffic to the website or not, thus increasing it's value immensely.

Organic, natural traffic sent directly from search engines is the best kind, however back links from other websites are also very important to potential buyers.

An easy way to determine the number of backlinks as well as page rank and other important information is by visiting www.CheckPageRank.net where you can enter in domain names and retrieve useful data relating to the name itself.

When it's time to register your domain names, you can use any registrar that you wish.

Personally, I use both www.NameCheap.com and www.GoDaddy.com , a favorite among the domain buyers and sellers. Regardless of the registrar you choose, you will want to make sure that you park them on service sites such as www.Afternic.com or www.Sedo.com so that you are able to generate revenue while you are preparing to sell the domain itself.

6) Spelling and Pronunciation

Is the domain name easy to say aloud? If your customer were to purchase the domain and build a business with this name, would they be able to easily brand it?

For example, domain names with double letters such as www.cashhour.com may often be mistaken for www.cashour.com, just the same, domains with odd spellings, hyphens or numbers would have to be clearly spelled out, or explained when someone is attempting to promote their website through word of mouth, rather than in print.

Consider this when registering domain names, and make sure that the names you choose will not be mistaken or misspelled by potential customers of yours, as well as the person who ultimately purchases it from you, otherwise it will experience a significant loss in perceived value.

When choosing your domain names, there will be many factors that come into play.

The type of audience you are catering to, the auction sites you are featuring them on, the price range you are expecting and so on.

There is no 'one way' to do this, and you will learn to become a better domain evaluator (and purchaser) from hands on experience. Using the guidelines above however, will help you maximize your efforts and minimize your costs (and losses).

Here are some other recommended domain registrars:

www.Moniker.com
www.Enom.com
www.Dotster.com

Profitable Domain Parking

Domain Parking is when you temporarily direct your domain name to a website, who in turn, will pay you for the traffic that is received who in turn, ends up clicking on the featured advertisements.

Two of the more popular choices amongst domainers is www.Sedo.com and www.Afternic.com

These two parking services have been around for many years and are both reliable in terms of payment and in providing accurate statistical data.

With Sedo, they will indicate whether the domain name you are parking has existing traffic, and of course if it does, you can price your domain name at a higher range.

Sedo also creates a domain name sale page for you, which visitors to the domain will see whenever they visit. This means that you can end up selling domain names by doing absolutely nothing if someone stumbles across your domain and sees it for sale on Sedo.

Of course, you can choose to deny their offer if you aren't happy with it or accept it for prompt payment from Sedo, who will take a percentage of your sale and pay you the rest.

To register for a free Sedo account, visit http://www.Sedo.com and click on the "Create Your Free Account" link to begin.

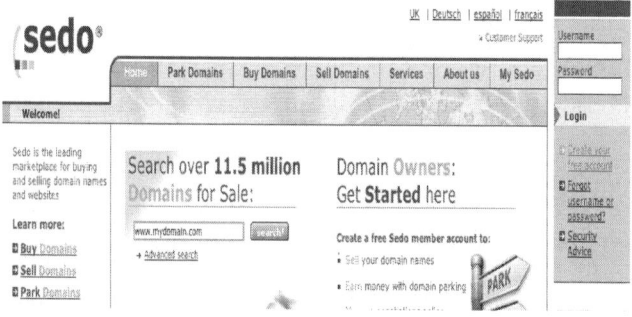

After you have created your account, Sedo will ask you to enter in any domain names that you wish to park with their service.

You can enter in as many or as little as you like, or you can skip this step altogether until you are ready to come back to it at a later time.

If you do decide to enter in domains at Sedo, you are able to specify a category, your asking price, and a minimum offer for each of your domains.

If you enter in a minimum offer, potential buyers

will be required to bid that amount in order to even be considered. This can save you a lot of time and eliminate ridiculously low bids of a few bucks.

I always enter my minimum bid to be at least $15 above my registration cost.

Here are a few reputable parking service providers:

www.Sedo.com
www.Parked.com
www.Fabulous.com
www.Bodis.com
www.NameDrive.com

In order to direct your domain to your parking service, you will need to update the nameservers associated with your domains.

By default, your nameservers will point to the main page of whatever domain registrar you choose, for example, if you register a domain name with NameCheap, your domain www.xyz.com when loaded, will bring visitors to NameCheaps' main page until you update the DNS.

It's quite easy to do this, and depending on your register the exact area in your account where you update this information will vary, however the best way to begin is first by creating your account on the parking service you choose to go with, such as www.Sedo.com .

Sedo will provide you with nameservers that may look something like this: ns1.sedoparking.com and ns2.sedoparking.com

After you have these nameservers written down, log into your domain account and search for the "NameServer Update" link (It may be called DNS update, Web Hosting Update, etc).

You may need to contact your domain registration provider to ask where to go about changing this information if you are unable to locate it within your account.

Shortly after you update the nameservers, your domain will be pointed to its new parking home, and you will be able to see this by entering in your domain name and seeing where it leads you.

If you update your nameservers and your domain still remains pointing to your registrar, don't panic-- it can take up to 24 hours for your domain's nameservers to be successfully updated, so check back at a later date to confirm that your domain name is now pointing correctly.

It's important to get to know your way around your domain registration interface because once you sell domains, you will need to transfer (or push) them to your customers.

For registrars such as www.NameCheap.com, you can click on the "Push Domain" link and enter in your customers username and instantly push the domain into their account, without them even having to accept.

For GoDaddy.com, transferring a domain name is a bit more complicated, as you will be required to enter in personal information regarding the customer who purchased the domain from you, but after you've done it a few times it will be extremely easy and quick to process each order as your domains sell.

Note: Don't be afraid to contact your domain registrar for assistance should you be confused about how to transfer domains, register domains or update your nameservers. They are there to help you, and with many of the more popular domain registration providers, they offer live help, toll free support and online help desk should you need to get in touch with a support representative.

The Value In Dropped Domains

Apart from expired domains, those that have been dropped with existing traffic and page rank are extremely valuable.

Using a service such as that of www.FreshDrop.net , you will be able to locate domain names with existing PR (Page Rank ranging from PR2-PR6, although PR2 and PR3 are the easiest to find).

PR, or Page Rank simply indicates that the domain was receiving traffic prior to expiring or dropping, and of course, online merchants place a lot of value on purchasing a domain that has already generated traffic, saving them the initial work of launching a domain, or waiting for it to be aged enough to appear in the search engines, not to mention the fact that domains with page rank carry more weight in the search engines such as www.Google.com .

There is also discussion involving new domain names being placed in what is referred to as a 'sandbox', where they are kept for a period of time before being released to appear in search engines, another reason why aged domains are so valuable to merchants.

At www.FreshDrop.net , you can browse through their search functions selecting to locate domains with specific PR.

Personally, I set the search tool to seek out domains with a PR of no less than 2. You can do this by clicking on the tab marked "EXP Name" and running your search query.

Finding decent domain names with existing page rank, isn't all that difficult and by featuring them within domain auctions on sites like NamePros.com, DNForum.com (paid membership) or Ebay.com can instantly generate a consistent income with little effort.

Once you have structured your system and are seasoned with doing your daily rounds of searching through domain listings, dropped and expired domains, and checking sites like Fresh Drop for domains with PR, you will find it incredibly easy to generate dozens of valuable domain names that you can quickly flip for profit.

It's an exciting business to be a part of, no doubt about it.

Backordering Domain Names

It's very difficult to rely on our ability to catch a domain name as it has dropped and register it before someone else does. Furthermore, most of the registrars don't even allow the better domains to be dropped, instead, placing them in online auctions.

This is where backordering comes into play.

With backordering services, you are able to pre-purchase a domain name that is about to expire, as long as the current owner fails to renew it themselves.

However, there is no guarantee you will be given the domain name, even if it expires due to other back ordering services offering the same opportunity to other people who are looking to snag a great domain name that's about to drop.

Still, it definitely increases your chances at being able to scoop up some of the better domain names with existing traffic and page rank.

Here are a few of the more popular back ordering services:

www.NameJet.com
www.SnapNames.com
www.Pool.com

Domain Flipping System

It's time to set up your domain names on eBay!

Before we do this however, there are a couple of important things to take into consideration:

1) If you are new to eBay, you should take some time to read their website and get to know how their auctions work, as well as the applicable fees and listing options.

2) You can lose a lot of money buying into the bells & whistles so avoid purchasing any add-ons when you list your domain names. You do not need a featured listing, a highlighted auction title, or any of that silly stuff.

3) Your feedback rating is very important with anything you sell on eBay, whether it's domain names or childrens toys. People judge you based on the feedback you have received so if you have any negative feedback, I would suggest creating a new eBay account.

If you are brand new to eBay, there is little you can

do to generate positive feedback quickly, other than to ensure that you follow through with your auctions, keep open communication with your buyers and be prompt when pushing your domain names after they have been purchased. Never make them wait more than 24 hours for their domain.

4) Open a Paypal account; it's almost required in order to sell on eBay these days. People prefer Paypal and it just makes things a lot easier.

You can open and verify a Paypal account within a couple of days, so do your best to set this up prior to listing your auctions.

5) Choose a relevant eBay username. Don't try to be trendy and pick some crazy sounding username, choose one specifically for domain and/or site flipping. Something like DomainExperts or DomainTrends would be just fine. If you end up not liking what you chose you can change it every 30 days.

When you list your auctions on eBay, you should start them all off at $.99. Do not place a reserve on these auctions, and do not add any restrictions or limitations of any kind.

Just set them up individually, and list them at $.99 each to start.

For beginners the idea of paying $8 for a domain name and listing it at $.9 is nerve wracking however with a lower start-up price, you will entice more bidders to participate and your auction will boost up in price quickly.

Once people become attached to the domain, they will create a bidding war against any other user who tries to take it away from them and you will see your auction soar as it gets closer to the end of the time, so don't be too nervous about losing money.

Note: If you have paid more than the basic registration of a domain name, meaning that you have purchased a domain name for more than $7-9, depending on what you paid for the domain you may want to start the auction off on a higher amount, just be aware that the lower the start up bid, the more activity it will receive.

By not listing a reserve fee you will also be able to list your domains on eBay at a lower cost, as eBay charges sellers a fee for including a reserve price.

You should also pay attention to eBay listing sales, which occur from time to time and feature reduced fee auctions.

Whenever you see one of these, list as many domains as you can and save yourself a bundle in listing fees.

I also do not recommend that you feature a BIN (Buy It Now) price either, as you may end up short-changing yourself if you list the BIN at a lower price than others are willing to pay. Let the auction determine its own price and run its course.

When selling your domain names on eBay, always choose a relevant category. Personally, I always use:

Computers & Networking - Web Domains & Services – Domain Names - .com

Also be sure to include a direct headline to your auction listing, which describes the domain name you are featuring. Include the domain name in full within your auction title (example: www.Domain.com not just domain.com)

And most importantly, ALWAYS include a domain "idea", something that can provoke thought and get potential buyers to consider the various options that are available to them when using the domain name:

Example:

www.BusinessLinks.com - Premium .com Directory Name

Within your listing you will be asked to enter in additional information including the Type (which is Domain Names), the extension (.com) and a brief description.

Always include the domain registrar, the age (unless it's brand new than do not include it), and utilize the free option to include a gallery picture just because research has shown that auctions showcasing a photo of any kind will receive more attention.

(For pictures, you could search for domain related images on public domain sites or purchase a couple from a stock photo site such as www.DreamsTime.com)

When creating the body text of your listing, you want to provide as many ideas for possible use as you can, as well as giving them as much information relating to the auction as possible such as:

Payments Accepted and your terms (Payment is due within two days of auction, etc)

Transfer Time – How quickly you can push the domain over after payment is received, (I always include "Transfer Within 24 Hours Of Payment Receipt")

And a link to any other domain auctions that you currently have going. This is very important and it's a great way to inter-link your auctions and encourage multiple purchases from your buyers since they can purchase as many as they like and pay all at once with the eBay checkout system.

The link to your other auctions is available under "Sellers Other Items". Just right click and choose "Copy Link" and create a new link in your listing that links to one another.

This takes time but it's definitely worthwhile!

Also be sure to include how long the domain is registered for, so buyers can determine how soon they will be required to renew it.

There are a lot of buyers who will not purchase a domain name that is due to expire within two months, so if you have just registered the domain name, then be sure to emphasize the fact that it is only expiring in a years time.

When listing your auction you can choose the time frame in which it will remain active. I typically choose the 7 or 10 day auction plan.

Be sure that you are available on the day that your auction ends and that you answer any questions that you receive during the course of your auction (and you can expect a handful).

Also be sure to include contact information, a gmail account will suffice and is easy to manage. www.gmail.com

Once again, choose an email address that relates to the domain industry, but avoid "domain flipping", "domain flipper" or terms like that. PremiumDomains@Gmail.com or ValuableDomains@gmail.com will give a better impression to your potential buyers and will simply look more professional.

When someone purchases a domain from you, depending on the registrar that yo use, you may be required to obtain specific information from your buyer in order to push the domain into their account.

For NameCheap, all you need is the buyers NameCheap uername which is quick and simple, another reason I tend to use them for domain flipping.

With GoDaddy.com however, you are required to have more information available regarding your buyer and their GoDaddy account.

Simply create an email draft within your gmail account that thanks your buyer for their purchase and requests the information that you need. By doin this, you can simply copy and paste that email to each buyer after a successful sale and let them follow up with their information.

If using NameCheap be sure to include the fact that they must complete their NameCheap profile entirely or NameCheap will not allow incoming domain pushes.

It only takes a few minutes for them to fill out their profile, but it's required and will save you time from attempting to push a domain only to be told that the buyers profile is incomplete.

Once again, be sure to communicate with your

seller and push the domain to them as quickly as you can after you have received payment.

I would also recommend not accepting echecks from Paypal as they take time to clear and will delay the process and cause more work on your end by having to remember to check when it has cleared, etc.

And finally, be sure that your buyers pay you BEFORE you push the domain to them. This might be obvious to you but it needs to be said, as I have talked to many new domain flippers who push the domain immediately only to never receive payment. Once the domain is pushed over it's not always easy to get it back.

The most activity that will take place within your auction is during the last hour that it's available.

This is when the bidding wars start to happen and people attempt to outbid each other or snag it at the last minute.

Because of this, you want to pay close attention as to when your auction will end. If you list it on a 7 day auction plan, and you start the auction on a Saturday, it will end the following Saturday.

The problem with this is that the weekends tend to be slower online in general, and on eBay , I have also experienced fewer bids and less activity if my auction ended on either Friday night, Saturday or Sunday.

My suggestion is to make sure that your auction will end on a weekday, any weekday will do. I tend to use the 7 day auction plan and list on Mondays regularly, so I keep a schedule and routine going that is easy to follow (and remember).

Another important thing to remember is the times that your auctions will end in between one another.

For example, if I list two auctions on Monday and it takes me ten minutes in between listing them, they will expire ten minutes apart.

This isn't always wise because if you have one buyer interested in both auctions they may not have the time to focus on bidding on both.

Therefore, I suggest timing your auctions 15-30 minutes apart, meaning; create one.. go for a short break, come back and list the second and so on.

Domain Tasting

When it comes to registering a new domain name, you are able to test-drive it for up to five days.

During these five days, if you are unhappy with the domain name, you are able to request a refund from your registrar and they will place the domain name back into the public registry, where it will once again be available for registration.

This means that you can register a domain name at absolutely no risk to you – test it out – and if you find that it will be a difficult one to sell or promote, you can get your money back quickly and easily.

Knowing this, it can certainly open up the potential of registering a handful of domain names, evaluating their marketability and weeding out the ones that are not feasible while saving money in the process, rather than squatting on a ton of domains that you just can't seem to move.

Domain tasting should not be confused with domain kiting, which is the process of deleting a domain name during the five-day grace period and immediately re-registering it for another five-day period.

This process is repeated any number of times with the end result of having the domain registered without ever actually paying for it.

One word of caution however, is that Google has indicated that their Adsense program will consistently scour the databases for domain names that are repeatedly registered and then dropped, removing the domain names from the Adsense program if these domainers are generating an income through Adsense with the intention of requesting a refund every five days.

This means that you should use the ability to domain test wisely and legitimately.

These five days should be spent testing the waters, getting a feel for whether you believe the domain is a viable one and conducting market research to determine the profitability of the names that you select.

Accepting Payment For Domain Sales
When you sell your domain name, you will want to ensure that the transaction goes through successfully prior to handing over the domain name to your customer.

One easy way to manage domain sales, is by using an Escrow service, where a middleman works at managing the sale by accepting payment from your customer, and transferring it to you once they have verified that the domain name has been transfered over.

With Escrow, you will pay a fee for using their services and so it's recommended that you only use it with larger domain sales. The most popular of these services, being www.Escrow.com

Paypal will suffice for smaller domain sales.

Conclusion:
Final Tips and Advice

When registering a lot of domain names, it's wise to use coupons that will save you a few bucks on the registration process. It will quickly add up to thousands of dollars in savings.

One of the best sources for current coupons and discounts can be found at
http://www.RetailMeNot.com/

Just enter in the domain registrar that you are planning to register your domains with, and RetailMeNot will search its database to determine whether there are existing coupons available.

I have always found discounts on GoDaddy.com and NameCheap.com just by browsing RetailMeNot, and for the most part, many of these coupons never seem to expire, and those that do are quickly replaced with fresh offers, so be sure to make a habit of checking for coupons prior to registering your domains.

Another important thing to keep in mind is that with many registrars, you are not permitted to transfer domain names to another registrar for a period of time, even if you are unhappy with their service.

In the case of GoDaddy, you are allowed to push domains to your customers instantly, but are unable to transfer domains from GoDaddy to another domain registration service for a period of 60 days, so keep this in mind when selecting your chosen provider.

If you are just getting started in domaining, you might want a second opinion on the domain names you are considering purchasing.

Many new domain vendors will post their intended domains on domain based forums, such as www.namepros.com asking for evaluations and advice.

While this can be extremely helpful, be careful with listing domains that you have yet to purchase, as it just might end up registered by someone else viewing the forum, and seeing value in your domain.

You can however, post domains that you have already registered if you are looking for advice on what price to list it at, or what starting bid to accept on online auction sites.

There are many helpful domain communities online available to help you get started on the right foot.

Take advantage of this opportunity by being active

within these circles, and helping others as you become more experienced yourself.

There is yet another reason to participate in domain based forums, and that is to be able to purchase affordable domain names that can be sold on other marketplaces.

Most domain based forums, such as NamePros.com, www.DomainState.com and DNForum.com categorize their domain sales into different groups, such as "Domain Auctions", where interested parties can bid on domain name.

"Domain Fixed Price", where domain names are sold at specific rates and the first one to pay the requested price claims it, as well as "Domain Offers", where domain holders are requesting offers on their portfolio of domain names, most of which may take place privately.

And finally, be careful when purchasing domain names from forums where the price just seems too good to be true. Often times, vendors will sell domains after they have been banned by Google (for breach of terms, including falsifying page rank, participating in link farms, breaking Adsense terms of service, etc).

You can easily validate the any domain name you are considering purchasing hasn't been banned by visiting www.SelfSEO.com or www.IWebTool.com and entering in the domain name.

To your domain flipping success!

Tools & Resources

Domain Suggestion Tools:
http://www.NameBoy.com
http://www.DomainFellow.com
http://www.DomainScour.com

Expired Domains (with PR):
www.DopeDomains.com

www.Exody.com - paid domain service, but well worth it. You will be provided with raw listings of expired domain names as well as domains that are current on hold or in redemption period.

www.ReadableDomains.com
www.DomainNameSoup.com

Domain History Tool:
http://domain-history.domaintools.com/

Expired Domains
http://www.ExpiredDomains.com
Free as well as membership options.

FreshDrop
http://www.FreshDrop.com

Free tool to research domain names that have recently expired. It also features information relating to these domains such as page rank, domain age and search engine listings.

SnapNames
http://www.SnapNames.com

Domain Name Generator
http://www.domainpunch.com/products/dnapro/

Domain Suggestion Tool:
http://domain-suggestions.domaintools.com/

Domain Suggestions, Expired Domains and more:
http://www.domainsbot.com/

NameBoy
http://www.nameboy.com

Domain Forums:

NamePros: http://www.NamePros.com

DN Forum: http://www.DNForum.com

Domain State: http://www.DomainState.com

Digital Point: http://forums.digitalpoint.com

Site Point: http://www.SitePoint.com

Flippa: http://www.Flippa.com

Domain Forum: http://www.DomainNameForums.com

Domain Forums: http://www.DomainForums.com

Domain Registrars:

Moniker – http://www.Moniker.com

Made in the USA
San Bernardino, CA
22 June 2013